Faith and Works

Foundations – Faith Life Essentials
Faith and Works

© 2009 Derek Prince Ministries–International
This edition DPM-UK 2019

ISBN 978-1-78263-542-0
Product code: B103D

DPM
Derek Prince Ministries
www.derekprince.com

EXPANDED
VERSION:
GROUP
STUDY

Faith and
Works

DPM

DEREK PRINCE MINISTRIES

Contents

About this Study Series.. 7

Faith and Works – an Introduction 11

Part 1 - Faith and Works.. 15

Part 2 - Righteousness before God.. 27

Part 3 - Law and Love 51

About the Author... 71

About This Study Series

The Bible is God's Word and our "instruction manual" to find the path to salvation in Jesus. It then shows us how to walk with Him once we have come to know Him. Logically, therefore, it is a hugely important part of our challenge as Christian believers to study the Word of God.

A sad fact is that very often we forget most of what we have heard quite quickly! As a result, what we have heard often has little impact on the way that we continue to live.

That is why we developed these Study Guides. As Derek Prince has said numerous times in his teaching, "It is a general principle of educational psychology that children remember approximately 40 percent of what they hear; 60 percent of what they hear and see and 80 percent of what they hear, see and do."

This Study Guide is intended to help you to assimilate the truths that you have heard into both your head and into your heart so that they become more than just knowledge and will begin to change the way that you live.

Living the Christian life

This study is part of a series of 10 messages, based on the doctrinal foundation of the Christian life described in Hebrews 6:1-2 which says,

Therefore, leaving the discussion of the elementary principles of Christ, let us go on to perfection, not laying again the foundation of repentance from dead works and of faith

toward God, of the doctrine of baptisms, of laying on of hands, of resurrection of the dead, and of eternal judgment.

This mentions six specific foundation stones that we need to lay before we can build a dwelling place for the Lord in our hearts and lives:

1. Repentance from dead works
2. Faith towards God
3. The doctrine of baptisms – John's baptism, Christian baptism and baptism in the Holy Spirit
4. Laying on of hands
5. Resurrection of the dead
6. Eternal judgment.

When this teaching is applied in your life, with faith, we believe that it will deepen your relationship with God and enable you to live a truly successful Christian life.

How to Study

Each book contains a QR-code (or DVD) that links you to a talk by Derek Prince, the transcript of the talk and questions for personal application or to be discussed in a group setting.

Each video is about an hour long, divided in three parts. Set aside a reasonable length of time to read the Introduction, then watch or read Derek's teaching, and finally come back to the Study Guide to reflect on the Study Questions or to discuss them with your study group.

Once you have completed this series you will find that you have an excellent summary of the teaching. This will help you to share the content with others, whether to a friend, home group or congregation. The more you share the truths you are learning, the more they will become part of your own life and testimony.

Group Study

This study guide has been developed for use by small groups as well as by individuals.

Simply proceed through the material as a team, reflect on the questions and explore the statements together for a rich and rewarding experience.

Scripture to Memorize

In this book, we have chosen key Scriptures for memorization. They will relate in some way to your overall study. Memorizing them will place a spiritual sword in your hands which you, by the Holy Spirit, will be able to use in times of spiritual conflict.

The Word of God has supernatural power for those who will take the time and effort to "hide it in their hearts" by memorizing and meditating on it. As God's Word is hidden in your heart, it becomes constantly available to you for reference, comfort, correction and meditation. Put simply, it becomes part of your life.

Look up the verse in your own Bible and write it in the space provided. You will want to write and say this verse out loud several times until you are confident you know it well. Take time to meditate on the words and their application to your life. As a group, you could talk briefly about the meaning of the verse and its relevance to the lesson or share how you applied it.

You will be asked to recall your Memory Work at the end of the book.

Faith and Works
– an Introduction

In this study, Derek Prince teaches about the extremely important, yet seldom understood, relationship between faith and works.

True faith is always preceded by true repentance, a change of mind and a change of direction. When the Bible talks about "dead works", it is referring to those actions that are not done as a result of our faith and obedience. They are not necessarily sinful things but God has not ordained us to do them.

However, though some might argue otherwise, Christianity is not a set of rules! We are not saved by works - rather true, living faith produces works of obedience in us – with the ultimate goal being love.

If that love is your motivation and desire in life, you're a totally free person because you can always do what you want. You can always love people. They may snub you, they may persecute you, they may even try to kill you, but they cannot stop you loving them. The person whose motivation is love is the only totally free person in the world.

Be aware of the trap of legalism and the desire to be made righteous independent from God. Pray for a fresh revelation of the completeness of Christ's work before you start this study and grow in your understanding of the place faith and works have in your life.

Watch the Derek Prince video teaching *Faith and Works* on YouTube. Scan the QR-code or visit dpmuk.org/foundations

This video is divided into three sections following the chapters in this book. You will find the links to these sections when you tap the 'down arrow' to expand the information about the video.

Write down these verses and try to memorize them.

Titus 3:5

He saved us not because of righteous things we had done but because of his mercy. He saved us through the washing of rebirth and renewal by the Holy Spirit.

Romans 6:14

For sin shall not be your master because you are not under law but under grace.

If you want your faith
to be counted to you for
righteousness, what is the
first thing you must do?
Stop working!

Faith and Works

Faith and Works is a theme to which Paul devoted an entire epistle—the epistle to the Galatians. Paul emphasized that a proper understanding of this topic was absolutely critical for their spiritual survival; and I believe it is no less serious for us today.

"Faith toward God" is the second in the list of Christian foundational doctrines enumerated in Hebrews 6:1–6:

1. Repentance from dead works
2. Faith toward God
3. The doctrine of baptisms (plural)
4. The laying on of hands
5. Resurrection of the dead
6. Eternal judgment

In our previous study, Through Repentance to Faith, we considered certain biblical aspects of true faith.

First, repentance must precede true faith. Repentance is a change of mind followed by a change in our actions or the direction of our lives. It is basically a change from trusting in ourselves and acknowledging the lordship of Jesus Christ over our lives.

Second, we considered four aspects of true faith.
1. Faith relates to the unseen. The Scripture tells us, "We walk by faith, not by sight" (2 Corinthians 5:6). If we can see, we don't need faith. Therefore faith is always tied to the unseen realm.

2. Faith is primarily character. Faith is not a matter of proper doctrine or emotional fervor. Faith comes from the heart and it is a matter of continuing on, or being "faithful" to believe the words of Jesus.
3. Faith brings confession. True faith will lead us to speak with our mouths that which we believe to be true. Jesus, as the High Priest of our confession, will only function as our High Priest in that which we confess.
4. Faith will be tested. Faith that is not tested is of no value to God. We should approach the testing of our faith with joy—not with dread. Why? Because God is working something of great value in us—the gold of true faith.

Turning to our topic of faith and works we first see these are two simple words that are used very commonly in the New Testament. Yet it is truly amazing how many of God's people do not have a clear understanding of the relationship between faith and works. By faith we mean simply "that which we believe." By works we mean simply "that which we do."

This study will primarily deal with the correct relationship between what we believe and what we do.

The Gospel of Jesus Christ

Many of us use the phrase "the gospel" as if we knew clearly what we were talking about. In fact, though people speak about the gospel, they are not aware of exactly what the gospel is. The gospel is stated very clearly by Paul in 1 Corinthians:

> *Moreover, brethren, I declare to you the gospel which I preached to you, which also you received and in which you stand, by which also you are saved, if you hold fast that word which I preached to you—unless you believed in vain.*
> *1 Corinthians 15:1–2*

Then Paul goes on to state the gospel as three simple historical facts:
For I delivered to you first of all that which I also received: that Christ died for our sins according to the Scriptures, and that He was buried, and that He rose again the third day according to the Scriptures, and that He was seen by Cephas, then by the twelve.
verses 3–5

The gospel consists of three simple historical facts: Christ died for our sins, He was buried, and He was raised again the third day. If these statements are not made, the gospel is not preached. Much contemporary so-called "gospel preaching" never actually contains the gospel. It may contain a great deal of truth and wonderful preaching, but if it does not contain these three basic facts, according to Paul, it is not the gospel.

To believe the gospel, we must lay hold of these vital facts: Christ died for our sins, He was buried, and He was raised again the third day.

Please note that the first attesting authority to Jesus' resurrection (given in verse 4) is not the eyewitnesses who saw Him after He was raised, but "the Scriptures."

The Scriptures are the ultimate authority. Paul says twice "according to the Scriptures" (verses 3, 4), and then he goes on to list various people who were eyewitnesses of Christ's resurrection. But bear in mind, as we saw clearly in our previous study, that the final authority in all matters of faith is the Scriptures.

Paul declares in 1 Corinthians 15:1–2 that if we will receive these simple facts by faith, we will be saved. Furthermore, Paul is very clear that when we receive the gospel by simple faith, without works, righteousness will be imputed to us; that is, He will count us as righteous. God Himself will declare us righteous. It is very important to see that Paul says it is not by what we do, but it is by what we believe. Not by works, but by faith.

Not by Works

In Romans 4 Paul discusses the lesson that we can learn from Abraham's faith. It says that Abraham's righteousness was imputed to him by faith and not because of any works Abraham performed.

> *What then shall we say that Abraham our father has found according to the flesh? For if Abraham was justified by works, he has something to boast about, but not before God.*
> *For what does the Scripture say? "Abraham believed God, and it was accounted to him for righteousness." Now to him who works, the wages are not counted as grace but as debt.*
> *Romans 4:1–4*

In this passage Paul presents a lesson about faith and works which we learn from the testimony of Abraham. If you work for somebody and receive your wages, it is not grace, but that which is owed to you. But Paul says we do not achieve righteousness by our works. Righteousness is not something we can earn.

Paul then makes the most amazing statement in verse 5. If you have never been surprised by what you read in the Bible, you have never really read the Bible. Paul's statement here should amaze us if we truly think about it:

> *But to him who does not work but believes on Him who justifies the ungodly, his faith is accounted for righteousness.*
> *verse 5*

If you want your faith to be counted to you for righteousness, what is the first thing you must do? Stop working! "To him who does not work." As long as you think you can earn righteousness by what you do, you will not receive it.

This is the hardest truth for religious people to grasp, because they are used to the idea of having to do something to earn God's favor. But, by definition, favor and grace cannot be earned. The first thing we have to do if we want to be reckoned righteous by God is stop trying. Do not work. This is a startling statement to many people, but the Bible is a startling book.

Relationship between Faith and Works

The real relationship between faith and works is defined by the order in which they come: first faith, then works. It is not that works are unimportant, but they follow true faith. They never precede it. Consider Paul's statement about faith and works in Ephesians 2:

> *For by grace you have been saved through faith, and that not of yourselves; it is the gift of God, not of works, lest anyone should boast.*
> *Ephesians 2:8–9*

We cannot even boast about the fact that we had faith for salvation. We only had that faith because God gave it to us. Faith is not something we can produce from ourselves. Paul says here that salvation cannot come from any form of works because they are rooted in human effort, which will ultimately foster pride on our part.

In many places Scripture speaks about people who believe they have been made righteous by their works. But Paul says God has not allowed righteousness to come through works lest they should boast. A religion of works fosters human pride, which is the great basic sin. God ordained a way of being made righteous that does not promote pride.

Consider the people who have rather complicated religions. Basically, the more difficult the religion is, the prouder the people become. They are doing something very difficult: fasting, sacrificing, and so on, which will ultimately foster pride. "God resists the proud, but gives grace to the humble" (James 4:6). God has devised a way that we might be found righteous with Him that does not promote our pride.

Perhaps you have noted that Christians who are very legalistic, insisting on keeping all the rules, often are not very loving people. If you go to them for love, you might not get much because, in reality, legalism and love are more or less opposites. We have to be on our guard continually against anything that would nurture pride, which religion usually does. If it is religion without the grace of God, it nurtures pride.

We must remember, though, there is a place for works. They are not unimportant. We just need to get faith and works in the right order. After this declaration of grace apart from works, Paul then explains the place of works in Ephesians 2:10:

> For we are His workmanship, created in Christ Jesus for good works, which God prepared beforehand that we should walk in them.

God created us anew in Christ: "If anyone is in Christ, he is a new creation" (2 Corinthians 5:17). God then has appropriate works prepared for each new creation. But the old carnal nature cannot walk in the good works that God has prepared. We have to be created anew by faith before we can walk in the good works. Once we are new creatures, then the good works become extremely important. But we have to get the order right. First is the new creation through faith; then the good works that God has prepared for us follow.

You may never have realized this, but you really do not need to work out what you should do for God. If you have become a new creature in Christ, God has already worked it out. What you have to do is find out the works God prepared for you beforehand. Don't try to make your own plan for your life. Find out what God's plan is. Many times, it is very different from what we would expect.

Let me give you a brief example from my own experience. I was an only child which meant, of course, I had no sisters. I grew up in exclusively all-male boarding schools from age nine to age twenty-five. I hardly had any contact with girls except for a few girlfriends. Basically, girls were a mysterious entity; I had no idea how to relate to them. But after God called me, I married a lady who had a children's home. The day I married her, I became the adoptive father to eight girls! You would never have thought that was the appropriate path for Derek Prince. If I had planned my own life that would never have been a possibility. But it was the good works which God prepared beforehand for me to walk in.

I find satisfaction in knowing that basically—though I have failed many times—I have walked in the good works which God prepared for me. I must honestly say that the life God prepared for me was far more wonderful and exciting than anything I could have ever made up on my own. This is why becoming a new creation through faith must come before we can encounter God's works for us. His works are always far better than anything our carnal nature could come up with.

Study Questions

1. What special insights did you gain from this lesson?

    ----

2. In your own words, explain the relationship between what you believe (faith) and what you do (works).

    ----

3. When people are confronted with the gospel, they often say: "But I'm not that bad. I'm actually a good person! I do my best to live a good, honest life. I'm giving to charity, I help my neighbor with her shopping...". What would your response to that be, based on what you have learned through this study?

----

4. Read Romans 3:20, 4:1-4, and 11:6. According to Paul, righteousness is not something we can earn. Why not?

----

5. Read Galatians 3:1-13. Think of areas where we, as Christians, might be in danger of trying to be 'made perfect by the flesh'. Ask the Holy Spirit to reveal to you where this applies in your own life.

----

7. When you are a new creation, you no longer need to work out what you should do for God – He has already prepared those works in advance. What part do we play in this?

----

6. Meditate on Romans 4:5: God justifies the ungodly. Write down any thoughts that come to your mind. Take time to praise God for His abounding grace.

As you finish the first part of this study, ask for God's help to apply the truths from this study practically in your life.

SUMMARY

- The gospel is comprised of three simple, historical facts (see 1 Corinthians 15:1-5): We are justified, or reckoned righteous, when we believe these three facts.
  - Jesus was delivered up to death on account of our sins.
  - Jesus was buried.
  - God raised Jesus on the third day.

- We receive righteousness as a result of what we believe (faith) and not on what we do (works) (Romans 4:2; Ephesians 2:8-10).

- Though righteousness comes by faith, living faith goes on to produce appropriate works (see James 2:24,26).

- We are not required to keep the law of Moses – or any other law – to be righteous before the Lord. Christianity is not a set of rules.

- Rather than bringing us righteousness and life, the Law actually brings condemnation and death because we are unable to keep it – the problem is not with the Law, but in us. (Romans 7:5, 1 Corinthians 15:56)

- Even though we are not saved by works, they are still very important - we simply need to get faith and works in the right order. (Ephesians 2:10)

Law and grace are
mutually exclusive.
You cannot benefit from
both; it has to be one
or the other.

Righteousness before God

We now need to define grace, and it requires some clear thinking. In fact, we really need clear thinking all the time!

Grace is a beautiful word, but it is often abused. I was preaching once in a certain church and I said, "As a matter of fact, the churches that call themselves 'Grace' churches often know the least about grace." Then I realized that I was preaching in one of those churches! Nevertheless, it remains true and I have to stand by that statement.

A lot of people who use the word grace have no idea what it really means. One of the meanings of grace is "comeliness," which means "beauty." It is beauty that God imparts to us because we believe in Him. He makes us beautiful with His grace.

Paul says:

> *If by grace, then it is no longer of works;*
> *otherwise grace is no longer grace.*
> *Romans 11:6*

I would say it like this: "You cannot earn grace. Anything you can earn is not grace." This is somewhat humbling for many of us. We have to depend on God's grace; we cannot earn it. Nothing we do can ever obtain for us the grace of God. We can never deserve the grace of God, because if we deserved it—it wouldn't be grace!

"By grace we have been saved through faith"
(Ephesians 2:8).

Then, just when we are getting excited about the fact that we have faith, Paul goes on to say, "And that not of yourselves; it is the gift of God" (verse 8). We have nothing whatever to boast of if we have been saved by faith. God has done this to protect us from the greatest sin of all—pride.

Now, let's consider the relationship between faith and works— what we believe and what we do. As far as I know, what I am writing is taken directly from the New Testament. Yet, for many, it will be startling and even shocking. I have discovered that merely preaching the simple New Testament message of salvation by grace is startling to most professing Christians.

I remember once saying to a congregation, "Of course, Christianity is not a set of rules." When I looked at those people, they were shocked. I think they would have been less shocked if I had said, "God is dead." Their concept of Christianity was that it was a set of rules.

Maybe you have the same concept. I want to tell you, Christianity is not a set of rules. You cannot achieve righteousness by keeping laws and regulations.

The theme of Romans is righteousness—essentially, how we can become righteous before God. Many, many centuries before the book of Romans was written, Job had cried out in his agony, "How can a man be righteous before God?" (Job 9:2). His religious friends all ridiculed the idea that anybody could ever be righteous before God. But God heard Job's cry, and many years later, through the epistle to the Romans, God answered the question— and it was not by keeping a set of rules as Job's friends would have led him to believe. Paul says of keeping rules to be righteous:

Therefore by the deeds of the law no flesh [human being] *will be justified in His sight, for by the law is the knowledge of sin.*
Romans 3:20

This is the translation taken from the New King James Version; and the New International Version translates it essentially the same. But both of them insert two words that are not there in the original Greek. The translators put in the word "the" before the word "law" both times it is used: "the law." But the actual words of Paul are: Therefore by the deeds of law no flesh will be saved, for by law is the knowledge of sin.

Therefore, Paul is not referring to just the Law of Moses, but to all law, all rules or anything that would define what we should do to obtain righteousness on our own. If law cannot make us righteous, then what was the purpose of the Law?

The Law was God's diagnostic to expose our problem—sin. The Law can diagnose our problem, but it cannot solve it. It can only be solved by grace. We need the Law to get us to the point where we see that we need grace. That is the purpose of the Law.

James says:
For whoever shall keep the whole law [he is talking about the Law of Moses], *and yet stumble in one point, he is guilty of all. For He who said, "Do not commit adultery," also said, "Do not murder." Now if you do not commit adultery, but you do murder, you have become a transgressor of the law.*
James 2:10–11

You either keep the whole Law or you do not keep any of the Law. To keep ninety-nine percent of the Law is not to keep the Law. The Law is one whole system.

None of us can keep the Law anywhere near ninety- nine percent. The Orthodox Jews say there are 613 commandments they need to observe. Privately, they will admit to observing no more than about 32 of these. No one alive on the earth today keeps the entire Law of Moses. No one has ever done so, except one: Jesus. He said to the people of His day, "Which of you convicts Me of sin?" (John 8:46). They could not answer Him. He is the only one who kept the Law perfectly. You and I cannot do it.

When I was in the British army and was saved, I began to talk to people about salvation. I discovered, however, as soon as I began to speak about it they all began to think in terms of religion, not salvation. I found, generally speaking, each one of them would trot out a little list of rules that he kept. That was his righteousness and it was especially tailored to his own situation. If he was involved in some wrongdoing, he would not include that rule in his list.

This is how the human mind thinks, "I am righteous by keeping a set of rules." No, we are not! We could be, if we kept the whole law all the time. But we don't—we can't.

We cannot keep just a small portion of the law and think that is all that is needed, because the law is one single system. We either keep it or we do not keep it. If we could keep it all, God would consider us righteous. But, we cannot. We find ourselves shut up to the only alternative, which is grace—something we cannot earn.

Returning to Romans 3:20: "Therefore by the deeds of law no flesh will be justified in His sight." We can never achieve righteousness with God by keeping a set of rules. We can only fail. If our rules are right, we cannot keep them. If our rules are wrong, we might be able to keep them, but we cannot be made righteous by keeping wrong rules.

Law and Grace—Mutually Exclusive

Many people are completely shocked when they learn that law and grace are mutually exclusive. You cannot benefit from both; it has to be one or the other. Romans 6:14 says:

> *For sin shall not have dominion over you, for you are not under law but under grace.*

These are two mutually exclusive alternatives. You can be under law or you can be under grace. But you cannot be under both law and grace at the same time. If you are under law, you are not under grace. If you are under grace, you are not under law.

The implications of what Paul says are very far-reaching. He says, "Sin shall not have dominion over you, for you are not under law but under grace." The implication is that if you are under law, sin would have dominion over you. The only way to escape from the dominion of sin is to stop trying to keep a law and avail yourself of God's grace. This realization can be shocking and you yourself may be a little bit shocked as you read this.

In Romans 8:14, Paul says:

> *"For as many as are led by the Spirit of God, these are sons of God."*

Who are the real children of God? Those who are led regularly by the Holy Spirit. Being led by the Spirit of God is the alternative to keeping a set of rules. We can keep a set of rules or we can be led by the Holy Spirit, but we cannot do both.

Here is a simple illustration which usually makes this concept vivid. In this illustration we find a young man who has just graduated from a Bible school. He has a degree in theology and he is strong and healthy. As his graduation exercise God presents him with the challenge of making his way on foot from where he is to a certain destination. God says to him, "Now, you have two alternatives. You can either use the map or you can avail yourself of a personal guide."

The young man thinks, "I'm pretty smart. I have a degree in theology. I know how to read maps." So he says to God, "I'll take the map; I don't need the guide."

When he starts off, the sun is shining and the birds are singing. But after three days of travel, it is the middle of a cloudy night and he is deep in a forest. He finds he is on the verge of a cliff, and he does not know whether he is facing north, south, east or west. Then a gentle voice says to him, "Can I help you?" Do you know who that is? It is the Holy Spirit, the personal Guide.

So the young man says, "Holy Spirit, I really need You!" The Holy Spirit takes him by the hand, leads him through the darkness, out of the forest, and onto a clear path where they start off on the road again.

After a little while the young man says to himself, "That was a bit silly! I could have handled that without any help. I really didn't need to panic." Even as he says it, he looks around and his Guide is no longer there. He is on his own.

Three days later, he is in the middle of a bog. With every step he sinks deeper and he sees only more bog in every direction. A gentle voice says to him, "Perhaps you need Me now?"

"Oh, Holy Spirit, please help me! Only You can get me out of this." So the Holy Spirit leads him to firm ground and sets him on a path towards his destination. Then he says to the Holy Spirit, his Guide, "I have an excellent map here. Maybe I could share it with You?"

The Guide says, "Thank you, but I don't need the map; I know the way. Besides, it was I who made the map!"

How long will it take before we realize we cannot find our way on our own? We cannot attain righteousness by our good works, by keeping rules: it comes only by the Holy Spirit, the Spirit of grace. "As many as are [regularly] led by the Spirit of God, these are sons of God" (Romans 8:14).

Led by the Spirit

In Galatians 5, Paul continues this theme, which is one of the major themes of the New Testament. Anybody who has not learned to walk by the Spirit of God is in a twilight state. Many Christians live in a kind of twilight— halfway between law and grace—because they do not know which is which nor how to avail themselves of God's grace. Paul says:

> *"But if you are led by the Spirit, you are not under the law."*
> *Galatians 5:18*

Paul said in Romans that "as many as are led by the Spirit of God, these are sons of God" (Romans 8:14). So we have a choice. We can live like sons of God and be led by the Holy Spirit, or we can turn our backs on the Holy Spirit and try to keep the law. But, we cannot combine the two. This is the essence of much of Paul's message in the New Testament. This is where people get into the twilight state. They are half trusting in grace and half trusting in their own little set of rules that they are trying to keep.

It is not necessarily a bad thing to keep rules. But keeping rules does not make us righteous. Please understand: keeping rules does not make us righteous. Most of us belong to some kind of church denomination, or at least a type of church—each one having its own set of rules. If we belong to a particular group, we ought to keep the rules. If we cannot keep the rules, we should not belong. But, keeping the rules does not make us righteous—it merely makes us a member of the group.

In fact, these sets of rules are really a major source of division in the body of Christ because most religious groups have their own set of rules which they believe makes them more righteous than the other groups. The Catholics have one set of rules, the Baptists another, the Seventh Day Adventists another, the Charismatics another, and so on.

Most of the people in the different groups think that keeping their rules makes them righteous. Then, they look at the people who keep a different set of rules and say, "Well, they are not really righteous because they are not keeping our rules." Thus legalism becomes a major source of division in the body of Christ.

Each denomination is free to keep its own rules— provided they are scriptural. But bear in mind, none of the individuals in these groups are made righteous by keeping these rules. Each one is made righteous by faith. If, however, we get focused on rules, we will probably miss out on faith and find ourselves in the twilight again. Or, we will end up like the young man who thought he could find his way by using the map and ended up in a bog.

As you read this, you may know what it is like to be in a bog. Not only that, but you may also know from personal experience that the Holy Spirit has gotten you out of a bog.

The Law Stirs up Sin

Romans is a most wonderful book—a very logical book. I was a professor of logic before I became a Christian. I was fascinated by logic and I think logic is a wonderful tool. It is somewhat like a computer. If you feed the right information into it, you will get the right results. But if you feed in the wrong information, you will get the wrong results. Logic does not give the answers. It merely enables us to see if the conclusions are compatible. As a logician, I would say to myself, "Of all the things I have ever read, the Bible is the most logical book—and Romans is one of the most logical books in the Bible." I do not feel intellectually inferior because I believe the Bible. That is my personal attitude and I would suggest that you should not feel intellectually inferior either. When you truly understand the Bible and the logic of God, it is one of the most logical and intellectually consistent books ever written.

Paul is using some profound logic when he makes another shocking statement, one I would not dare to make if Paul had not made it first. It is found in Romans 7. (The further you go with Paul, the more shocking he becomes!)

> *"Therefore, my brethren, you also have become dead to the law through the body of Christ, that you may be married to another—to Him who was raised from the dead, that we should bear fruit to God."*
> *Romans 7:4*

Paul says that at one time, if you were a religious Jew, you were married to the Law. For you to depart from the Law and be married to somebody else would be adultery—spiritual adultery—unless you found out that the Law had been put to death. But through the death of Jesus on the cross, the whole system of law was brought to an end.

This is a real problem for most Jewish people. Religious Jews feel that if they do not try to keep the Law (and basically they don't do that very well) they are being unfaithful to their "husband." Jews, and most Christians I might add, must come to a revelation that the Law was put to death in Christ so that they could be married to another— the risen Messiah. Then, through Him, both they and we bring forth fruit works, which God has prepare beforehand. Fruit only comes by union. What we are united to will determine what we bring forth. If we are united, or in union, with Christ, then we will bring forth the fruit of the Spirit. If we remain united with the law, we will bring forth the fruit of death. As Paul says:

For when we were in the flesh, the sinful passions which were aroused by the law were at work in our members to bear fruit to death. Verse 5

This is an amazing statement! The passions of sin were aroused by the law. In other words, Paul says, the law stirred up the sinful passions. Can you absorb that? Law never produces righteousness. It produces more sin!

In 1 Corinthians 15:56, Paul makes another one of these breathtaking statements.

"The sting of death is sin, and the strength of sin is the law."

Paul is saying that sin's strength, or power, comes from the law. Do you understand what that means? The law actually gives power to sin. This is why trying to keep the law will never overcome our sin. Why? The more we try the keep the law the more power we give to sin. It is a losing battle. Trying to keep the law bears fruit for death. Paul goes on in Romans 7 to say there is nothing wrong with the law. It is "holy and just and good" (verse 12). The problem is not in the law, the problem is in us.

Let me put it like this: law works from without. It says, "Do this; don't do that." We then decide what we will or will not do. In doing so, we are trusting in our own ability. That is the problem. In ourselves, we do not have the ability to do what is right and avoid what is wrong. The essential nature of our flesh is to trust in ourselves. Our flesh does not want to depend on God.

Sin—Independence From God

Let's consider the temptation in the Garden of Eden. What was the motivation that Satan used? "You will be like God" (Genesis 3:5). There is nothing wrong with being like God. What was the problem? They would be like God without depending on God. They would depend only on the knowledge of good and evil.

That is the root problem of humanity; it is also the root problem of religious people. We want to be like God, but we do not want to depend on God. The essence of sin is the refusal to depend on God. Sin is not necessarily some particular sinful act we commit, but it is an attitude of self-reliance that shuts out God's grace from our lives. This is the hardest flaw God has to deal with in you and me—this attitude of self-righteousness. "I can do it by myself. I don't need God."

As far as I know (and this is just my opinion), there are only two kinds of creatures in the universe that wanted to be independent of God. One is the fallen angels that joined Satan in his rebellion, and the other is the human race. Nothing else in the universe desires to be independent of God. Neither the birds, the creatures, the fish nor the stars desire to be independent. They are all happily dependent on God.

But you and I, because of the fall and our fleshly nature, have inherited this problem: we do not like to depend on God. We like to be able to say, "I've done it by myself, and I didn't need God."

The fact is, we need God in the worst way, and most of all when we think we do not need Him. If we analyze our own Christian experiences, I think we will find that every problem we ever encounter stems from trying to do something without God. Our failures originate from the refusal to depend on the grace of God.

Some years ago, Ruth was in a weakened state in a Catholic hospital awaiting surgery. She wanted to read her Bible but she couldn't. She didn't have the strength. The senior nun in that hospital, who was well over 70, was going around visiting the new patients when she saw Ruth. Ruth's Bible lay open, but she was unable to read it. This dear sister said, "Is there anything I can do for you?"

Ruth said, "Yes, would you please read the Bible to me?"

The sister replied, "What do you want me to read?" Ruth said, "Philippians 2."

The sister then commented, "Well, that was the Scripture on which I was consecrated as a nun." So they had something in common.

This Catholic sister then shared the following story with Ruth. She had attended a retreat for nuns at which the speaker was a Trappist monk. Trappists have a vow of silence, meaning they are not allowed to speak in their monastery. But when occasionally they are allowed to leave, they are then permitted to teach people what they have learned during their silence. This Trappist monk was teaching the Catholic sisters, and he shared something this sister passed on to Ruth. And what she shared had a profound impact on both of us.

Here was a monk who was not permitted to speak, teaching a little group of Catholic sisters. But his message then reached me and I have put it in my messages so often that it has basically reached the world! This really blesses me, because I see that if God wants something to get around, it will get around! Who could have planned that? Nobody but God. This is what the monk shared with the group of nuns: "Pray to desire not to be esteemed, not to be secure, and not to be in control."

Would you pray that? It takes a little doing, doesn't it? Think it over for a while. Not to be esteemed—I would not have a big problem about that. Not to be secure—I truly believe my security is in the Lord. But where the monk said to pray not to be in control, not to be independent—that would be the hardest one for me. Do I really desire not to be in control? In other words, am I really willing to let God be in control? That is the issue. That's grace, when God is in control.

I bless that dear nun, and I thank her for what she contributed to my thinking.

The Desire for Independence

I see this desire as the basic problem of humanity— our desire to be esteemed, to be secure and to be independent. The essence of sin is this: to be in a universe that was created by a loving, all-wise God and yet to want to be independent of Him. None of us has consistently been content to depend on God and to let Him be in control. It is a real walk of faith, a walk of grace. We cannot achieve it in a few hours.

Returning to the law, we see that the law stirs up this inclination to be independent of God. Why? Because the law says, "Go ahead, rely on yourself. You can do it! All you have to do is keep the rules." The law tricks us into self-reliance and self-dependence. In so doing, it deceives us.

Let me emphasize again, there is nothing wrong with the law. Paul stated in Romans 7 that the law is good, holy and righteous (Romans 7:12). The problem is in us—in our fleshly nature, which has a desire to be independent. Most people have observed a baby at one time or another. At about two years old, this very desire to be independent comes to the top. You may say to this sweet little toddler, "Come here," and she turns around and walks in the opposite direction! That is the old carnal nature manifesting itself. The law is God's diagnostic to bring that problem out into the open.

Here is a simple illustration of the reason for the law. If you were to go to the doctor with a stomach ache, a good doctor would never just hand you a box of tablets. He will first try to find the cause of your stomach ache. In other words, before he prescribes a remedy, he will seek a diagnosis. That is also how God deals with us. He does not offer a remedy until He has diagnosed the problem. The law is His diagnostic tool. The law is given by God to convince us of the source of our problem, which is sin. Once we believe the diagnosis, we need to know what the remedy is.

In Romans 10:4, we read:

For Christ is the end of the law for righteousness to everyone who believes.

When you become a believer in Jesus Christ, it is the end of the law. Not the end of the law in every sense, but the end of the law as a means for righteousness. Christ put an end to the law as a means of achieving righteousness with God. When Christ died, He fulfilled the law and put an end to it. When He rose from the dead, He offered us a new way of being righteous with God—what is known as living by faith. This was not the end of the law as a part of the Word of God or as a part of the history of Israel or as an example of the way that God deals with people. The law is still there. But as a means to achieve righteousness, the death of Christ on the cross finally put an end to the law.

MY NOTES

Study Questions

1. What special insights did you gain from this lesson?

   ----

2. In your own words, how would you describe the essence of sin? Would you agree this is the root problem of humanity?

   ----

3. What happens when a person becomes prideful? List some results. Is there a difference between pride and self-esteem?

---

4. What is grace? Describe it in your own words. Take time to thank God for His grace working in your life.

---

5. Reflect on Romans 11:6 and compare it to Jeremiah 17:5-10. Our hearts are deceitful, making us want to rely more on our own efforts than on God's grace. Do you recognize the tendency to trust yourself more than to trust God? What feelings or thoughts are keeping you from trusting Him?

---

6. If the Law cannot make you righteous before God, then what was the purpose of the Law? Do Christians not have to obey the Law?

---

7. Some people think Christianity is a set of rules. What is the alternative?

---

8. Reflect/Discuss: Derek Prince says: "Most of the people in the different groups think that keeping their rules makes them righteous. Then, they look at the people who keep a different set of rules and say, "Well, they are not really righteous because they are not keeping our rules." Thus legalism becomes a major source of division in the body of Christ." What are your thoughts on this?

---

9. Ask the Holy Spirit to reveal where your church (or you personally) needs to repent from spiritual pride or legalism.
Pray for your church and the other churches in your area to find unity in the Spirit of God, and to be free from legalism.

----

10. Reflect/Discuss: The root problem of humanity and of religious people is that we want to be like God, but we do not want to depend on God. The essence of sin is the refusal to depend on God. Sin is not necessarily some particular sinful act we commit, but it is an attitude of self-reliance that shuts out God's grace from our lives. Are there areas of your life where you struggle to depend on God? Do you see this as sin?

----

11. Philippians 2:12-13 contains an apparent contradiction. How can we be responsible to 'work out our salvation', if God is the One working in us for His own pleasure?

Before closing this chapter, why not commit this area of growth to the Lord and ask Him for His grace to help you?

SUMMARY

- According to Galatians chapter 3, returning to law and the works of the flesh brings us under a curse (Galatians 3:10).

- Law works from without, leaving us to our own ability whereas grace works from within, supplying us with supernatural ability.

- In Leviticus 11:44 in the Old Testament and 1 Peter 1:16 in the New Testament, we are told to "Be holy" as God is holy. The Law says, "I must keep all these rules"; Grace says, "Jesus in me lives out His holiness through me." (see 1 Corinthians 1:30 and Hebrews 12:10)

- Law and grace are exclusive of one another (Romans 6:14). Grace is received without earning it, and works refers to what we do.

- The Law can diagnose our problem, but it cannot solve it. We need the Law to get us to the point where we see that we need grace.

- Being led by the Spirit of God is the alternative to keeping a set of rules.

- The essence of sin is the refusal to depend on God. It is not necessarily some particular sinful act we commit, but it is an attitude of self-reliance that shuts out God's grace from our lives. The root problem of humanity (and of religious people) is they want to be like God, but do not want to depend on God.

- Fruit only comes by union. What we are united to will determine what we bring forth. If we are united, in union with Christ, then we will bring forth the fruit of the Spirit.

We do not receive the
baptism in the Holy Spirit
by keeping a set of rules,
but by faith.

Law and Love

The Galatian Error: The Problem of the Law

In Paul's letter to the Galatian Christians he deals extensively with the problem of the Law. In theological terms, the problem was legalism. Galatians is an interesting epistle. In most of the letters Paul wrote to churches, he began with a glowing thankfulness to God for all the good that they have demonstrated. Even the Corinthian church, where there was a man living with his father's wife and where there was drunkenness at the Lord's Table, Paul begins with a glowing expression of his gratitude to God for God's grace.

But when he wrote to the Galatians, he was so hot under the collar that he did not spend time thanking God for His grace. What was the problem with the Galatians? Not drunkenness nor immorality but legalism. Paul viewed that as a much more serious threat to their well-being than immorality or drunkenness.

Please understand, I do not believe that God condones immorality and drunkenness. But I believe those are much easier problems to deal with than legalism because legalism is so subtle. Since legalism appears to be so good, it is hard for us to be delivered from it. Paul says:

> "I marvel that you are turning away so soon from Him who called you in the grace of Christ, to a different gospel, which is not another; but there are some who trouble you and want to pervert the gospel of Christ."
> Galatians 1:6–7

Paul had nothing good to say to this church. He simply said, "I'm amazed you turned away so quickly." Turned to what? Into legalism—into keeping a set of rules and believing they could be made righteous by keeping them.

In chapter 3, Paul returns to this theme:

"O foolish Galatians! Who has bewitched you...?"
Galatians 3:1

There is no question that Paul was writing to Charismatic believers who were filled with the Spirit of God.

Years ago, I remember reading this verse and suddenly realizing that "Evangelical" or "Charismatic" Christians could be bewitched. It solved a big problem in my mind because it explained to me a situation that had arisen in a church I was then pastoring. I saw that my whole congregation had been bewitched by the wife of the previous pastor who had divorced her husband and married one of the board members while continuing to dominate the congregation spiritually.

Legalism Bewitches

Paul uses the word bewitched with a very clear meaning. Actually, the Greek word for bewitched means "to strike with the eye." This church had been smitten with the eye; they had come under the gaze of an eye that bewitched them. In the case of the Galatians, they had come under the dominating gaze of Jewish law which brought spiritual deadness. A Greek Orthodox priest who had become Charismatic contacted me years ago. He came to me for prayer, saying, "I've been bewitched. Somebody has put the evil eye on me." He was a very sober man and he knew his Bible. I prayed for him and he was set free. I want you to be aware that being bewitched is a possibility. In fact, in some places it is a probability. So let me just offer this advice: If you are dealing with some problem in a church you cannot understand, it may be that the people have been bewitched. It is possible for an entire church to come under the controlling, dominating gaze of an individual which will produce spiritual deadness, fear and confusion.

> *"O foolish Galatians! Who has bewitched you that you should not obey the truth, before whose eyes Jesus Christ was clearly portrayed among you as crucified?"*
> *Galatians 3:1*

Paul says, in effect, "I presented you the message of the cross. I depicted to you Jesus crucified for our sins. How can you have been moved away from that to some other basis of righteousness?"

> *"This only I want to learn from you: Did you receive the Spirit* [the Holy Spirit] *by the works of the law, or by the hearing of faith?" Verse 2*

In other words, Paul asks: "Were you baptized in the Holy Spirit because you kept a set of rules or because you heard the message and received it with faith?"

Let me ask you the same question: Is there anyone who has been baptized in the Holy Spirit as a result of keeping a set of rules? The answer is: no one. We need to bear in mind that we are not saved by keeping a set of rules. We do not receive the baptism in the Holy Spirit by keeping a set of rules.

We received the Holy Spirit, as Paul says, by the hearing of faith. We listened to the message, we heard it with faith, we believed it, and we received it. That is always the biblical pattern: listen, hear, believe, and receive. There is no place for our own effort or works in this pattern.

> *"Are you so foolish? Having begun in the Spirit* [the Holy Spirit], *are you now being made perfect by the flesh?" Verse 3*

When Paul puts it that way, it sounds stupid, doesn't it? If we need the Holy Spirit to start on the pathway of righteousness, how can we ever cease to be dependent on the Holy Spirit? How can we ever rely on our own little set of rules? But this is a very real problem in too many churches and among too many believers.

The Law Brings a Curse

Paul goes on in Galatians 3:

> *"For as many as are of the works of the law are under the curse; for it is written, "Cursed is everyone who does not continue in all things which are written in the book of the law, to do them." verse 10*

As we have seen, if we are going to be justified by keeping the law, we must keep the whole law all the time. If we try to keep the law but do not keep the whole law all the time, we come under the curse pronounced here: Cursed is everyone who does not keep the words of this law all the time. Is it possible for Evangelical and Charismatic believers to come under a curse? It is very possible. It is a fact which I know from experience.

Years ago I was part of a movement in the body of Christ which was initiated by the Holy Spirit; a work that none of us who were involved could have anticipated. God joined me together with three other preachers, all of whom were fairly well known. It was a sovereign act of God. We began in the Spirit, but we were not going very long before we had ended in the flesh. The results were disastrous. I know this is real. It happened to me. God, by His grace, got me out of it.

The reality of a curse is not something from the remote past. It is still happening today. People who begin in the Spirit and then try to be made perfect by the flesh come under a curse.

Trusting in the Flesh

Consider Jeremiah 17:5:

Thus says the Lord: "Cursed is the man who trusts in man and makes flesh his strength, whose heart departs from the Lord."

Because it says, "his heart departs from the Lord," it is clear that such a man had a relationship with the Lord. But after he entered that relationship, he began to trust in man, himself. And as a result, his heart departed from the Lord.

I think this has happened to the majority of the professing Christian Church. Most of the significant denominations or movements in the Church were brought into being by a sovereign work of the Spirit of God through His grace. They would have never amounted to anything apart from the sovereignty of God. But how many of them today are continuing in the grace of God? I would say very few. They have brought themselves under the curse pronounced in Jeremiah 17:5: "Cursed is the man who trusts in man and makes flesh his strength." Let me illustrate this from a personal experience.

Ruth and I decided to sell our house in Jerusalem and we went to the real estate brokers who assured us, "It's a beautiful house; you'll sell it quickly." For fourteen months it did not sell. We could not understand it. Then one Sunday Ruth and I were at a service in Christ Church (the church we attended in Jerusalem), and the rector there said he had to pray with a man who needed deliverance from evil spirits. Not all rectors talk like that—but this one did—that is one reason why we liked him! So we thought we should try and help him.

We went with the rector to visit the man for whom we would be praying. He was a missionary from Africa who had come under a curse pronounced by an African bishop. The man was nearly dying. We ministered, and the man was delivered from a number of evil spirits.

Then we began to deal with this man's whole attitude toward life. I said, "It seems to me you are really trusting in yourself and you are not really relying on the grace of God. As a matter of fact, I've had that problem, too." I never planned to say this—it just came out. But I heard myself saying, "I've had that problem because in selling our house I've been trusting on what I could do. I've been relying on myself."

Ruth, with characteristic frankness, said to me in front of all these people, "Then you're under a curse."

I said, "That's right; I am." So I confessed it, repented of it, and released myself from the curse. We left the meeting, drove back to the new apartment where we were living, and on the ground floor we met a real estate agent who said, "I would like to show your house to some customers I have." Within two weeks the house was sold! Do you understand? The moment I was free from the curse brought on by trusting in the flesh, God could move on our behalf.

Be Holy

Let me summarize and then we will look at the positive. It bears repeating that law works from without, leaving us to our own ability. Grace works from within, supplying supernatural ability. We can only live victoriously in Christ by grace.

In both Leviticus 11:44 and 1 Peter 1:16 we have the commandment, "Be holy." This is a commandment from God in both the Old and New Testaments.

In Leviticus 11, this command comes at the end of an elaborate set of rules about what we may or may not eat. The implication is if we are going to be holy we must keep all these rules.

However, in 1 Peter 1 the command is not attached to any set of rules. The message is simply, "Be holy." It is a message from Jesus: "Let Me live out My holiness in you." It is totally different. We need no longer rely on our own efforts, but on the grace of God and Jesus to do what we cannot do for ourselves. We have the choice.

The Righteous Requirement of the Law

In Romans 8 we begin to consider the positive side of the requirement to be righteous. Take note that Paul says here that there is nothing wrong with the law. What is wrong is our weakness.

> For what the law could not do in that it was weak through the flesh, God did by sending His own Son in the likeness of sinful flesh, on account of sin: He condemned sin in the flesh, that the righteous requirement of the law might be fulfilled in us who do not walk according to the flesh but according to the Spirit.
> Romans 8:3–4

This raises the all-important question: What is the righteous requirement of the law? Have you ever considered this? The answer is one word of four letters: love. Love is the righteous requirement of the law, and we will see this through a number of Scriptures.

In Matthew 22, Jesus was asked a question by a lawyer—and you know what the legal mind is like. He asked a specific question, and Jesus gave an immediate, specific answer.

> Then one of them, a lawyer, asked Him a question, testing Him, and saying, "Teacher, which is the great commandment in the law?"
> Jesus said to him, "'You shall love the Lord your God with all your heart, with all your soul, and with all your mind.' This is the first and great commandment. And the second is like it: 'You shall love your neighbor as yourself.'"
> Matthew 22:35–39

The key word is love: love for God and love for our neighbor.

Then Jesus commented, "On these two commandments hang all the Law and the Prophets" (verse 40).

To illustrate this, if I were getting overheated, I would want to take off my jacket and hang it up. But I would need a hook or peg to hang it on. The hook would need to be there before I could hang my jacket on it. Jesus said these two commandments are the hook on which the whole law and the prophets are hung. In other words, when we have read the whole law and the prophets, what it says is that we should love God and love our neighbor. That is the righteous requirement of the law.

Obligation to Love

Then in Romans 13, Paul says:

Owe no one anything except to love one another,
for he who loves another has fulfilled the law.
Romans 13:8

I believe in being out of debt, but there is one debt I can never get out of: To love my fellow Christians and to love my fellow human beings. I owe that. I am continually in debt to that obligation; I cannot get out of it.

Paul goes on:

For the commandments, "You shall not commit adultery,"
"You shall not murder," "You shall not steal," "You shall not bear
false witness," "You shall not covet," and if there is any other
commandment, are all summed up in this saying, namely,
"You shall love your neighbor as yourself." Love does no harm to
a neighbor; therefore love is the fulfillment of the law.
verses 9–10

In Galatians 5 Paul states this again:

For all the law is fulfilled in one word, even in this:

"You shall love your neighbor as yourself."
Galatians 5:14

Faith and Love

Back in verse 6 of Galatians 5 Paul had said:
For in Christ Jesus neither circumcision nor uncircumcision avails anything, but faith working through love. verse 6

How does faith work? Through love. James says it this way:
Faith without works is dead.
James 2:26

Since faith works by love (Galatians 5:6) and faith without works is dead (James 2:26), then we find this equation: Faith without love is dead. That is a shocking statement, but it is true. You can claim to have all faith, but if there is no love in your life it is a dead faith (See 1 Corinthians 13:2).

We read in 1 Timothy 1:
Now the purpose of the commandment is love from a pure heart, from a good conscience, and from sincere faith, from which some, having strayed, have turned aside to idle talk.
1 Timothy 1:5–6

The New American Standard Bible says, "The goal of our instruction is love." When I read that, I say to myself, "Is that really the goal of my instruction? Am I really aiming to produce loving people?"

When I think of some of the people who have sat under my ministry, I sometimes wonder if I have imparted love. Essentially, I am a teacher, and a teacher imparts knowledge. But Scripture tells us that knowledge "puffs up" (1 Corinthians 8:1). Knowledge makes people proud. I try, by all the means in my power, to teach without producing pride in people. The goal of our instruction must always be love.

Growing in Love

Then Paul adds that if we stray from that goal, all we are doing is "idle talk." Let's contemplate the Church as we know it. How much idle talk goes on there? How much of our preaching, teaching, and activity does not produce love? If it does not produce love it is all wasted effort; it is totally ineffective.

If you are involved in any kind of ministry, I want to challenge you to analyze your motives. What are you aiming to produce? And secondly, if you are aiming to produce love, are you producing it? If you are not aiming to produce love, all your talk is just empty words. That is a far-reaching statement.

Law motivates through fear, but Jesus motivates us through love. He says, "If you love Me, [you will] keep My commandments" (John 14:15). Fear does not produce the right results. There are many religions, including some professing forms of Christianity, that motivate people by fear. They produce the most terrible results.

Finally, I want to point out that the obedience of love is progressive. Are you perfect in love? Join me; neither am I perfect in love. However, even though I have not yet fulfilled the love requirement of the law, that does not mean I am not accounted righteous. Until we achieve the goal of love, as long as we continue believing, our faith is accounted to us for righteousness. (See Romans 4:5.) This is wonderfully exemplified by the words of Jesus to Peter at the Last Supper. He said, "Peter, you're going to deny Me three times."
Peter said, in effect, "Not I. Never."
And then Jesus said, "But I have prayed for you, that your faith should not fail" (Luke 22:32). The really important thing is that our faith does not fail. We may make many mistakes; we may even commit sins. After all, we have not arrived; we are not perfect. But as long as we continue believing, our faith is accounted to us for righteousness until we arrive.

Love Brings Freedom

I will close with a Scripture from James, which I love.

But he who looks into the perfect law of liberty and continues in it, and is not a forgetful hearer but a doer of the work, this one will be blessed in what he does.
James 1:25

What is the perfect law of liberty in one word? Love. If we love—really love—we are totally free, because we can do whatever we want.

We can always love people. They may snub us, persecute us, or maybe even try to kill us. But they cannot stop us from loving them. The person whose motivation is love is the only totally free person in the world.

PRAYER

Father, help me to understand that righteousness is received by grace from You by faith. It is not worked out by what I can do. Help me to trust in You and not in my own strength.

I affirm that Jesus in me lives out His holiness through me. My faith confirms my love for You and my love for my neighbor.

I love You, Lord, and I thank You that my faith, and not my performance, is reckoned as righteousness before You.

Amen.

Study Questions

1. What special insights did you gain from this lesson?

   ----

2. Read Galatians 3:1-3. Paul says the Galatian Christians were bewitched. In your own words, what did he mean by that? What does it produce?

   ----

3. Read Galatians 3:10 and Jeremiah 17:5. Is it possible for a Christian to come under a curse? How?

----

4. Reflect and pray about Jeremiah 17:5: *Cursed is the man who trusts in man and makes flesh his strength.*
Does this apply to any areas in your life?

----

5. Derek Prince describes a situation where he was under a curse himself. How did he know he was? How did he respond?

----

6. Read Matthew 22:35-39 and Romans 13:8-10. What is the key requirement from God's Law?

    ----

7. Reflect/discuss: Romans 13:8 says there is one debt you can never get out of: to love your fellow Christians and to love your fellow human beings. How does love fulfil the Law?

    ----

8. Read Galatians 5:6 and James 2:26. Why is faith without love dead?

    ----

9. Derek Prince states that any activity in church that does not produce love, is wasted effort. If you are involved in any ministry or activity in your church, analyze your motives. What are you aiming to produce?

----

10. "The person whose motivation is love is the only totally free person in the world because you can always do what you want. You can always love people. They may snub you, they may persecute you, they may even try to kill you, but they cannot stop you loving them."
What does it mean to love people? Is this motivation to love something we need to receive from God, or is it something to develop? What could be helpful in this process?

Ask the Lord to give you a deep and true understanding of the completeness of Christ's work.

As you conclude this lesson on Faith and Works, ask the Lord to help you to cement this part of the foundation stone firmly so that you do not turn back to law and the works of the flesh as a means to righteousness.

PRAYER

Loving Father, I recognize anew my need for Your grace. Jesus, I pray that You would live out Your holiness through me and that Your gift of grace would work from within me - supplying me with supernatural ability.

I am enabled to love because I have come to experience Your love for me. I ask that You would heal me of my insecurities and empower me to freely give of the love that You have so freely given to me.

Having seen how the Law brings me under bondage, I choose the perfect law of liberty, I choose faith and I choose to walk in the good works that You have prepared in advance for me to do.

In line with the Trappist monk's prayer, I pray for the desire not to be esteemed, not to be secure and not to be in control. It seems so far beyond where I am today but I see the need for total dependence on You, that You would be my all in all and that I would be delivered of the need for honor, security and control outside of You. I commit myself afresh to You today in unreserved obedience. Amen.

Remember that with all of the suggested prayers through this course, the words are clear and intentional, but they are also designed to provide a catalyst for you to pray what is on your heart. Scripture tells us to pray without ceasing so when you read the word "Amen," you don't need to stop praying. Prayer needs to become a lifestyle and these written prayers are simply here to help you on that pathway.

- Love is the righteous requirement of God's law. (Matt 22:35-39, Romans 8:3-4)

- The goal of our instruction (teaching) and church activity should always be love. (1 Timothy 1:5)

- Law motivates us through fear but Jesus motivates us through love. He said, "If you love me you will keep my commandments." (John 14:15)

- The perfect law that brings liberty is love. (James 1:25)

The next study, *The Doctrine of Baptisms*, explains the three different forms of baptism presented in the Bible. What made John's baptism different from the Christian baptism? What is required in order to be baptized?

Recall and write down the verses you memorized
at the beginning of this book:

Titus 3:5

Romans 6:14

About the Author

Derek Prince (1915–2003) was born in India of British parents. He was educated as a scholar of Greek and Latin at Eton College and King's College, Cambridge in England. Upon graduation he held a fellowship (equivalent to a professorship) in Ancient and Modern Philosophy at King's College. Prince also studied Hebrew, Aramaic, and modern languages at Cambridge and the Hebrew University in Jerusalem. As a student, he was a philosopher and self-proclaimed agnostic.

Bible Teacher

While in the British Medical Corps during World War II, Prince began to study the Bible as a philosophical work. Converted through a powerful encounter with Jesus Christ, he was baptized in the Holy Spirit a few days later. Out of this encounter, he formed two conclusions: first, that Jesus Christ is alive; second, that the Bible is a true, relevant, up-to-date book. These conclusions altered the whole course of his life, which he then devoted to studying and teaching the Bible as the Word of God.

Discharged from the army in Jerusalem in 1945, he married Lydia Christensen, founder of a children's home there. Upon their marriage, he immediately became father to Lydia's eight adopted daughters – six Jewish, one Palestinian Arab, and one English. Together, the family saw the rebirth of the state of Israel in 1948. In the late 1950s, they adopted another daughter while Prince was serving as principal of a teacher training college in Kenya.

In 1963, the Princes immigrated to the United States and pastored a church in Seattle. In 1973, Prince became one of the founders of Intercessors for America. His book Shaping History through Prayer and Fasting has awakened Christians around the world to their responsibility to pray for their governments. Many consider underground translations of the book as instrumental in the fall of communist regimes in the USSR, East Germany, and Czechoslovakia.

Lydia Prince died in 1975, and Prince married Ruth Baker (a single mother to three adopted children) in 1978. He met his second wife, like his first wife, while she was serving the Lord in Jerusalem. Ruth died in December 1998 in Jerusalem, where they had lived since 1981.

Teaching, Preaching and Broadcasting

Until a few years before his own death in 2003 at the age of eighty-eight, Prince persisted in the ministry God had called him to as he traveled the world, imparting God's revealed truth, praying for the sick and afflicted, and sharing his prophetic insights into world events in the light of Scripture. Internationally recognized as a Bible scholar and spiritual patriarch, Derek Prince established a teaching ministry that spanned six continents and more than sixty years.

He is the author of more than fifty books, six hundred audio teachings, and one hundred video teachings, many of which have been translated and published in more than one hundred languages.

He pioneered teaching on such groundbreaking themes as generational curses, the biblical significance of Israel, and demonology. Prince's radio program, which began in 1979, has been translated into more than a dozen languages and continues to touch lives. Derek's main gift of explaining the Bible and its teaching in a clear and simple way has helped build a foundation of faith in millions of lives. His nondenominational, nonsectarian approach has made his teaching equally relevant and helpful to people from all racial and religious backgrounds, and his teaching is estimated to have reached more than half the globe.

DPM Worldwide Ministry

In 2002, he said, "It is my desire – and I believe the Lord's desire – that this ministry continue the work, which God began through me over sixty years ago, until Jesus returns." Derek Prince Ministries International continues to reach out to believers in over 140 countries with Derek's teaching, fulfilling the mandate to keep on "until Jesus returns." This is accomplished through the outreaches of more than thirty Derek Prince offices around the world, including primary work in Australia, Canada, China, France, Germany, the Netherlands, New Zealand, Norway, Russia, South Africa, Switzerland, the United Kingdom, and the United States.

For current information about these and other worldwide locations, visit **www.derekprince.com.**

FOUNDATIONS
faith life essentials

www.dpmuk.org/shop

This book is part of a series of 10 studies on the foundations of the Christian faith.

Order the other books to get everything you need to develop a strong, balanced, Spirit-filled life!

1. Founded on the Rock
There is only one foundation strong enough for the Christian life., and we must be sure our lives are built on Jesus Himself.

2. Authority and Power of God's Word
Both the Bible and Jesus Christ are identified as the Word of God. Learn how Jesus endorsed the authority of Scripture and to use God's Word as a two-edge sword yourself.

3. Through Repentance to Faith
What is faith? And how can you develop it? It starts with repentance: to change the way we think and to act accordingly.

4. Faith and Works
Many Christians live in a kind of twilight - halfway between law and grace. They do not know which is which nor how to avail themselves of God's grace.

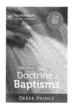

5. The Doctrine of Baptisms

A baptism is a transition - out of an old way of living into a totally new way of living. All of our being is involved. This study explains the three different forms of baptism presented in the Bible.

6. Immersion in the Spirit

Immersion can be accomplished in two ways: the swimming pool way and the Niagara Falls way. This book takes a closer look at the Niagara Falls experience, which relates to the baptism of the Holy Spirit.

7. Transmitting God's Power

Laying on of hands is one of the basic tenets of the Christian faith. By it, we may transmit God's blessing and authority and commission someone for service. Discover this Biblical doctrine!

8. At The End of Time

In this study, Derek Prince reveals the nature of eternity and outlines what lies ahead in the realm of end-time events.

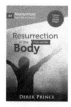

9. Resurrection of the Body

The death and resurrection of Jesus produced a change in the universe. Derek explains here how the resurrection of Jesus impacted man's spirit, soul, and body.

10. Final Judgment

This book examines the four major, successive scenes of judgment in eternity. Exploring the distinctive aspects of these four judgments, Derek opens the Scriptures to bring forth treasures hidden there.

Christian Foundations Course

If you have enjoyed this study and would like to deepen your knowledge of God's Word and apply the teaching – why not enrol on Derek Prince's Christian Foundations Bible Course?

Building on the Foundations of God's Word

A detailed study of the six essential doctrines of Christianity found in Hebrews 6:1-2.

- Scripture-based curriculum
- Practical, personal application
- Systematic Scripture memorisation
- Opportunity for questions and personal feedback from course tutor
- Certificate upon completion
- Modular based syllabus
- Set your own pace
- Affordable
- Based on *Foundational Truths for Christian Living*

For a prospectus, application form and pricing information, please visit www.dpmuk.org, call 01462 492100 or send an e-mail to enquiries@dpmuk.org

Foundational Truths For Christian Living

Develop a strong, balanced, Spirit-filled life, by discovering the foundations of faith: salvation; baptism, the Holy Spirit, laying on hands, the believers' resurrection and eternal judgment.

Its reader-friendly format includes a comprehensive index of topics and a complete index of Scripture verses used in the book.

ISBN 978-1-908594-82-2
Paperback and eBook
£ 13.99

www.dpmuk.org/shop

More best-sellers by Derek Prince

- Blessing or Curse: You can Choose
- Bought with Blood
- Life-Changing Spiritual Power
- Marriage Covenant
- Prayers & Proclamations
- Self-Study Bible Course
- Shaping History Through Prayer and Fasting
- Spiritual Warfare for the End Times
- They Shall Expel Demons
- Who is the Holy Spirit?

For more titles: www.dpmuk.org/shop

Inspired by Derek's teaching?

Help make it available to others!

If you have been inspired and blessed by this Derek Prince resource you can help make it available to a spiritually hungry believer in other countries, such as China, the Middle East, India, Africa or Russia.

Even a small gift from you will ensure that that a pastor, Bible college student or a believer elsewhere in the world receives a free copy of a Derek Prince resource in their own language.

**Donate now: www.dpmuk.org/give
or visit www.derekprince.com**

Derek Prince Ministries

DPM–Asia/Pacific
38 Hawdon Street
Sydenham
Christchurch 8023
New Zealand
T: + 64 3 366 4443
E: admin@dpm.co.nz
W: www.dpm.co.nz

DPM–Australia
15 Park Road
Seven Hills
New South Wales 2147
Australia
T: +61 2 9838 7778
E: enquiries@au.derekprince.
com
W: www.derekprince.com.au

DPM–Canada
P. O. Box 8354
Halifax
Nova Scotia B3K 5M1
Canada
T: + 1 902 443 9577
E: enquiries.dpm@eastlink.ca
W: www.derekprince.org

DPM–France
B.P. 31, Route d'Oupia
34210 Olonzac
France
T: + 33 468 913872
E: info@derekprince.fr
W: www.derekprince.fr

DPM–Germany
Söldenhofstr. 10
83308 Trostberg
Germany
T: + 49 8621 64146
E: ibl@ibl-dpm.net
W: www.ibl-dpm.net

DPM-Netherlands
Nijverheidsweg 12
7005 BJ, Doetinchem
Netherlands
T: +31 251-255044
E: info@derekprince.nl
W: www.derekprince.nl

ffices Worldwide

DPM–Norway
P. O. Box 129
Lodderfjord
N-5881 Bergen
Norway
T: +47 928 39855
E: sverre@derekprince.no
W: www.derekprince.no

Derek Prince Publications Pte. Ltd.
P. O. Box 2046
Robinson Road Post Office
Singapore 904046
T: + 65 6392 1812
E: dpmchina@singnet.com.sg
W: www.dpmchina.org (English)
    www.ygmweb.org (Chinese)

DPM–South Africa
P. O. Box 33367
Glenstantia
0010 Pretoria
South Africa
T: +27 12 348 9537
E: enquiries@derekprince.co.za
W: www.derekprince.co.za

DPM–Switzerland
Alpenblick 8
CH-8934 Knonau
Switzerland
T: + 41 44 768 25 06
E: dpm-ch@ibl-dpm.net
W: www.ibl-dpm.net

DPM–UK
PO Box 393
Hitchin SG5 9EU
United Kingdom
T: + 44 1462 492100
E: enquiries@dpmuk.org
W: www.dpmuk.org

DPM–USA
P. O. Box 19501
Charlotte NC 28219
USA
T: + 1 704 357 3556
E: ContactUs@derekprince.org
W: www.derekprince.org

Lightning Source UK Ltd.
Milton Keynes UK
UKHW021657130720
366461UK00005B/141